Let's Cook!

Mexico

Códices Indigenas Mexicanos

INGRESO A LA ESCUELA
(Códices Florentino)
RAMON ALCÁNTARA R.
MEXICO 1.60
T.I.E.V.

The Culture and Recipes of Mexico

Tracey Kelly

PowerKiDS
press™

Published in 2017 by
The Rosen Publishing Group, Inc.
29 East 21st Street, New York, NY 10010

Cataloging-in-Publication Data
Names: Kelly, Tracey.
Title: Culture and recipes of Mexico / Tracey Kelly.
Description: New York : PowerKids Press, 2017. | Series: Let's cook! | Includes index.
Identifiers: ISBN 9781499431858 (pbk.) | ISBN 9781499432657 (library bound) | ISBN 9781499431865 (6 pack)
Subjects: LCSH: Cooking, Mexican--Juvenile literature. | Food habits--Mexico--Juvenile literature.
Classification: LCC TX716.M4 K455 2017 | DDC 641.5972--dc23

For Brown Bear Books Ltd:
Text and Editor: Tracey Kelly
Editorial Director: Lindsey Lowe
Children's Publisher: Anne O'Daly
Design Manager: Keith Davis
Designer: Melissa Roskell
Picture Manager: Sophie Mortimer

Picture Credits: t=top, c=center, b=bottom, l=left, r=right. Front Cover: Shutterstock: sunsinger c, Morenovel r, Odua Images r, LanaN l, Brent Hofacker l, catwalker c, Noppasin t, milezaway t. Inside: 1, 123rf: Mike Flippo 15b, Wavebreak Media 30; Pilar Cantero: Identidades Mexico 23t; Dreamstime: 19b, 25br, Kobby Dagan 28-29c, 31br, Dieter Hawlan 9bl, Jesse Kraft 36-37t, Lunamarina 6b, Anna Omelchenko 5br, Arturo Osorno 11br, William Perry 28-29t, Juan Manuel Robledo 39, Travelling Light 45br, Martyn Unsworth 22t; Getty Images: Steve Dunwell 28-29b, Arturo Lara 20-21b; Shutterstock: 7b, 8-9t, 17b, 23b, 27br, 32bl, 37, AS Food Studio 1cl, Kobby Dagan 20-21t, 22b, Konstantin Kopachinsky 41b, Rafal Kubiak 5bl, Anamaria Mejia 5tl, Monkey Business Images 38-39b, Tyler Olson 25bl, Lefteris Papaulakis 1blr, Marco Regalia 7t, Nancy Sullins 1cr, 6t, T Photography 38-39t, Tati Novo Photo 36-37b, Lilyana Vynogradova 43br, Yeko Photo Studio 4l; Thinkstock: istockphoto 8cr, 10-11t, 19b, 30-31t, 33br, 35br.

Special thanks to Klaus Arras for all other photography.

Manufactured in the United States of America
CPSIA Compliance Information: Batch #BW17PK: For Further Information contact Rosen Publishing, New York, New York at 1-800-237-9932.

Contents

Looking at Mexico

Mexico is a country made up of 31 states. It is the 14th largest country in the world and home to over 120 million people—all of whom eat its delicious food!

Mexico is a country in North America. The United States forms its border to the north. Belize and Guatemala form its southern border.

Viva México!

Officially called the United Mexican States, Mexico is a long, bent, wedge shape of land with the Pacific Ocean to the west and the Gulf of Mexico and Caribbean Sea to the east. The country has dry deserts in the north, and major mountain ranges run up and down the length of the country. The tropical climate of the south is perfect for growing fruits and vegetables. Mexico has a long history with several great ancient civilizations, including the Olmec, Maya, and Aztecs. Spain overthrew the last of these, the Aztec Empire, in 1521. However, the descendants of these people make Mexico the beautiful and fascinating land it is today. Many of their delicious foods have conquered the world. Viva México!

A tortilla wrap stuffed with meat and colorful vegetables is a staple food in Mexico.

The land in northwest Mexico is mainly dry, barren desert. Cacti are among the few plants that grow here.

○ Tijuana

UNITED STATES

BAJA CALIFORNIA

SIERRA MADRE OCCIDENTAL

SIERRA MADRE ORIENTAL

Rio Grande

● Monterrey

La Paz ○
Mazatlán ○

MEXICO

GULF OF MEXICO

CUBA

○ Tampico   Chichén Itzá ○ ○ Cancún

Teotihuacán

Guadalajara ○   ○ **Mexico City**   YUCATÁN

○ Manzanillo   ○ Veracruz   **BELIZE**

PACIFIC OCEAN   ○ Palenque

Acapulco ○   ○ Oaxaca

GUATEMALA HONDURAS

Acapulco is a famous Mexican resort. Vacationers visit for its beautiful beaches, water sports, and restaurants.

Teotihuacán, near Mexico City, is one of many ancient ruins in Mexico. No one is sure who built it.

Desert Land

Hot, dry desert covers much of Mexico. Located in the central northern part of the country, the Chihuahuan Desert stretches across the border with the United States. It covers a large area of 175,000 square miles (450,000 square kilometers). The Chihuahuan Desert lies between the Sierra Madre Oriental and the Sierra Madre Occidental Mountains. Parts of it stretch into New Mexico and Texas. Other large deserts include the Coahuila Desert and Deserts of Nuevo León.

 Ocotillo flowers grow in the Chihuahuan Desert close to the Texas-Mexico border. Big Bend National Park, in Texas, forms the backdrop.

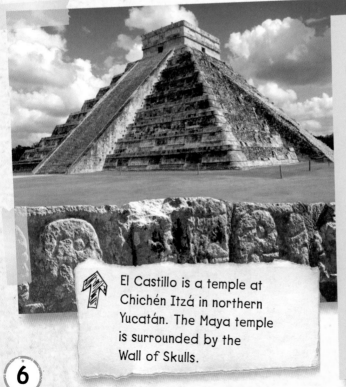

El Castillo is a temple at Chichén Itzá in northern Yucatán. The Maya temple is surrounded by the Wall of Skulls.

Ancient Sites

The Yucatán peninsula was home to the Maya, one of Mexico's ancient civilizations that began to develop in central Mexico around 1500 BC. The Maya left behind a legacy of temples, palaces, and plazas. Today, millions of people visit sites, such as the temples of Chichén Itzá, an astronomical observatory named El Caracol, and the Pyramid of the Magician at Uxmal. They also visit Palenque, a major Maya city in southeastern Mexico.

Popocatépetl is an active volcano that last erupted in 2016, spewing smoke and ash.

Mexican Plain

Much of Mexico's industry and food production take place in the Central Plateau (Plain), which is shaped like an inverted triangle. Moving south from the top, the land is fertile and supports farming for the area's dense population. The country's capital, Mexico City, is located here. It is one of the world's largest cities and sits in a basin 7,380 feet (2,250 meters) high. Surrounded by mountains, pollution from cars and factories hangs in a blanket over the city. Popocatépetl, an active volcano 17,802 feet (5,426 meters) high, is located only 43 miles (70 kilometers) away. Its name is the Aztec word for "smoking mountain."

Mountains High

Rugged mountain ranges border the Central Plateau: the Sierra Madre Occidental to the west and Sierra Madre Oriental to the east. They join together near Mexico City. In the southwest, mountains are covered with pine and oak forests that belong to Native Americans who have lived in the region for thousands of years. Oaxaca has stunning mountains, rivers, canyons, waterfalls, and lagoons.

Beautiful mountain views can be seen from the hot springs at Hierve El Agua, rock formations in Oaxaca, in western Mexico.

Food and Farming

Mexico produces plenty of fruit and vegetables, and its own staple—corn. People also rear cattle and catch fish.

Cacao and Corn

Corn and chocolate are among the top foods that Mexico has given the world! Centuries ago, Native Americans in Mexico farmed a wild grass named teosinte. Over time, they developed it into plump corn. Today, a favorite food is corn on the cob sprinkled with lime juice and salt, and grilled on a barbecue. Corn kernels can be dried and ground into masa harina flour, which is essential for making tortillas. The cacao tree is native to Central America. Aztec and Maya peoples made a hot drink by mixing the dark, bitter chocolate from its seeds with honey and spices, and so sweet chocolate was born! Spanish invaders took cacao seeds back to Europe, and chocolate spread across the world.

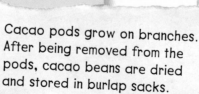

Cacao pods grow on branches. After being removed from the pods, cacao beans are dried and stored in burlap sacks.

Lush, green pastures make good grazing for livestock in a valley in Oaxaca, in southwestern Mexico.

Cattle Call

Mexico has a large amount of open grassland for herds of grazing animals. Cows, goats, and sheep are reared to produce dairy products and meat.

Animals are raised on the northern plain, in central Mexico, and in the south. The Spanish conquerors were the first to bring cattle, pigs, and horses to the country in the 1500s.

Today, cattle ranching is one of the fastest-growing industries in Mexico. The country produces and exports large amounts of beef, and Mexicans themselves eat many beef dishes. Sadly, forests are being cleared to create even more pastureland for grazing, and this is destroying the delicate habitats of many native animal and bird species.

Small Farms

Many farmers in central Mexico produce vegetables and fruit on small family farms. They grow corn, wheat, peanuts, chiles, squashes, and beans using traditional farming methods. People buy and sell produce at busy markets in every town and village. In the cities, huge markets like Mexico City's historic La Merced Market sell fresh food to thousands of city dwellers.

DID YOU KNOW?

Native American people have grown corn for around 10,000 years. From Mexico, corn spread north to the United States and south to Peru. It is now the world's most widely grown staple food.

Tropical fruits, such as bananas, pineapples, and peppers, fill a market stall with colorful, mouthwatering produce.

Tropical South

The south of Mexico and the Gulf Coast have a tropical climate, meaning that it is always hot and humid. Farmers grow coconuts, papaya, bananas, pineapple, and mangoes. Sugarcane, coffee, and cocoa beans are also important crops from the south, as well as the vanilla orchid, from which vanilla extract is made. Farmers in the Oaxaca region grow corn, beans, sugarcane, melons, and citrus fruit. In the lowlands of the Yucatán Peninsula, rice, wheat, squash, chiles, and tomatoes are grown, and beekeepers produce delicious honey.

A papaya plantation stretches across the foothills in Colima, a state in western Mexico on the Pacific coast.

Big Catches

With a vast 5,800 miles (9,330 kilometers) of coastline, fish and seafood are plentiful in Mexico. They are a key ingredient in the nation's cuisine. Along the coasts of the Gulf of Mexico, the Pacific Ocean, and the Baja Peninsula, fishermen catch lobster, shark, tuna, sardines, mackerel, and other fish and shellfish. Shrimp, sea bass, and shark are caught in the seas off the Yucatán Peninsula. Mexican fishermen catch around 1.6 million tons of fish and seafood each year, and three-quarters of this is fished near Pacific ports such as Manzanillo, Mazatlán, and Guaymas.

Fishermen bring in their catch on a beach near the port of Veracruz, in east central Mexico.

11

Let's Start Cooking

One thing's for sure—cooking is a lot of fun! In this book, you will learn about different ingredients, which tastes go together, and new cooking methods. Some recipes have steps that you'll need help with, so you can ask a parent or another adult. When your delicious meal is ready, you can serve it to family and friends.

This line tells you how many people the meal will feed.

Serves 4–6

In this box, you find out which ingredients you need for your meal.

Before you begin, check that you have everything you need. Get all the ingredients ready before you start cooking.

YOU WILL NEED

- 5 ounces milk chocolate or semisweet chocolate (or half of each)
- 2 large eggs
- 2 tablespoons confectioner's sugar

WARNING!

When to Get Help

Most cooking involves chopping ingredients and heating them in some way, whether it's frying, boiling, or baking. Be careful as you cook—and make sure your adult kitchen assistant is around to help!

TOP TIP

You can choose any chocolate you like.

Top Tip gives you more information about the recipe or the ingredients.

For many meals, you need to chop an onion. Cut a thin slice off at both ends, then pull off the papery skin. Cut the onion in half down the middle. Put one half, cut side down, on the cutting board. Hold it with one hand, and cut slices with the other hand. Hold the slices together, then cut across them to make small cubes. Be careful not to cut yourself!

Some recipes use fresh chiles—and they are very hot! Chile seeds and the white pith make your skin burn, so always wear rubber or vinyl gloves when chopping chiles. If you don't have any gloves, wash your hands really well afterward, and do not touch your skin or eyes for a while. To chop, trim the chile stalk, then halve lengthwise. Scrape out the seeds, and throw away. Slice the stalk into fine pieces.

METRIC CONVERSIONS

Oven Temperature		Liquid		Sugar	
°F	°C	Cups	Milliliters	Cups	Grams
275	140	¼	60	¼	50
300	150	½	120	½	100
325	170	¾	180	¾	150
350	180	1	240	1	200

Oven Temperature		Weight		Flour	
375	190	Ounces	Grams	Cups	Grams
400	200	1	30	¼	30
425	220	2	60	½	60
450	230	3	85	¾	90
475	240	4	115	1	120
		5	140		
		6	175		
		7	200		
		8	225		

Tasty Tortillas

Makes 12 tortillas

Tortillas are a great, versatile food. You can buy them at the store, but they are easy to make with this recipe. You can use them in many dishes.

YOU WILL NEED

- ✓ 2 cups masa harina flour
- ✓ a pinch of salt
- ✓ about 1½ cups hot water
- ✓ 1 teaspoon shortening

1 In a large bowl, mix the masa harina flour with the salt. Bring the water to boil in a saucepan, and pour it over the masa harina, stirring as you pour. Put the shortening in a skillet over medium heat, and stir until it is melted. Pour the shortening into the bowl with the flour.

2 Combine all the ingredients using a big wooden spoon. Be careful though: It's very hot! Put the bowl to one side, and leave the dough until it is cool enough to touch.

DID YOU KNOW?

Masa harina is a flour made from corn, available at most grocery stores. It is finer than cornmeal.

TOP TIP

To store tortillas, put them in a covered dish in the refrigerator for up to three or four days.

3 Using clean hands, knead the dough together, until it forms a big, doughy ball.

4 Divide the dough into twelve portions. To do this, first cut the ball in half, then cut each smaller ball in half again. Next, divide each of these four balls into three balls. Leave the dough balls for 1 hour.

5 Take a dough ball, and put it between two layers of plastic wrap. Then roll with a rolling pin, until you have a 6-inch (15 cm) circle. Pull off the plastic wrap, being careful not to tear the dough circle. Repeat with the other balls.

6 Heat the skillet, and add a tortilla. You don't need to add any fat. Cook for 1 minute, then turn with a spatula, and cook the other side for 1 minute. Cook all the tortillas. Cover them with a clean dishcloth to keep them warm, and serve.

Beef Wraps

Serves 4

Start these delicious beef wraps by cooking ground beef sauce. Then simply spoon onto tortillas, and add your favorite fillings!

YOU WILL NEED

- ✓ 1 large onion
- ✓ 1 garlic clove
- ✓ 2 small red chiles
- ✓ 3-4 fresh thyme sprigs
- ✓ 1 can (14 ounces) red kidney beans
- ✓ 2 tablespoons oil
- ✓ ½ pound ground beef
- ✓ 1 large can peeled and chopped tomatoes
- ✓ salt, pepper
- ✓ ½ teaspoon ground cumin
- ✓ tortilla wraps
- ✓ tortilla chips, to garnish

FOR THE FILLING:
- ✓ shredded lettuce
- ✓ grated cheese
- ✓ diced tomato
- ✓ chopped onion

1 Slice the top off the onion, peel, and chop it into small chunks (see page 13). Wash the garlic and chop.

2 Using a knife, slit the chiles open and deseed them (see page 13). Rinse the thyme sprigs, and pull the leaves off the stems. Chop them into fine pieces.

3 Carefully remove the lid from the can of kidney beans. Pour the beans into a colander placed over a big bowl. Rinse the beans in plenty of fresh, cold water, then let them drain in the colander.

4 Heat the oil in a large saucepan. Add the chopped onion, and fry over medium heat for about 5 minutes, until it is transparent (see-through). Stir the onion from time to time with a wooden spoon, so that it does not burn.

5 Add the ground beef to the pan. Squash larger pieces with the back of your spoon. Fry, stirring, until the meat turns from pink to brown.

6 Add the chiles, kidney beans, and can of tomatoes. Season with salt, pepper, cumin, and thyme. Stir everything to mix it well. Simmer the sauce for 30 minutes on low heat, stirring from time to time. Place a dollop of meat sauce in the middle of each tortilla. Top with lettuce, cheese, tomato, and chopped onion, and roll up the tortillas. Serve with tortilla chips.

TOP TIP

There are hundreds of different chiles. Some are very mild, others are extremely hot. Use only the amount a recipe calls for, so that you don't make your dish too hot to eat!

Guacamole

Serves 4

Guacamole is a scrumptious and creamy-smooth avocado dip. It can be eaten with tortilla chips, along with salsa and sour cream.

YOU WILL NEED

- ✓ 2 firm tomatoes
- ✓ 1 small onion
- ✓ 1 small red chile
- ✓ 2–3 ripe avocados
- ✓ 4–5 tablespoons lime juice
- ✓ a pinch of salt
- ✓ 1 handful of fresh cilantro

TOP TIP
Avocado flesh turns brown very quickly if it is not used. To prevent this, squirt some fresh lemon or lime juice all over the flesh.

1 Rinse the tomatoes under cold water. Cut them in half, and remove the stems. Using a spoon, scrape out the seeds, then chop the flesh into small cubes. Peel and chop the onion (see page 13), and chop the chile (see page 13).

2 Cut the avocados in half lengthwise, cutting all the way around. Twist the halves in opposite directions, so that they come apart. Carefully push the point of the knife into the pit, turn the knife, and pull out the pit.

3 With a tablespoon, scrape the avocado flesh out of the shells. Put the flesh in a blender with the lime juice, and blend. Add the tomato, onion, and chile. Season with a pinch of salt.

TOP TIP
Make your own chips by stacking a few tortillas and cutting them into wedges. Spread out the wedges on a baking sheet and leave for 30 minutes. Then put on a wire rack and bake in an oven preheated to 350°F for 15 minutes.

4 Wash the cilantro sprigs, and pat the leaves dry with some paper towels. Pull the leaves off the stems, and chop the leaves with a knife. Stir most of the chopped cilantro into the guacamole, and sprinkle the rest on top. Serve with tortilla chips.

National Festivals

Mexico has many national festivals. Some are religious, and some celebrate events in Mexican history, such as Independence Day.

Independence Day

The most important national holiday is Independence Day. It is celebrated on September 16, the day that Mexico remembers the fight to become an independent country. On September 15–16, 1810, a priest named Miguel Hidalgo rang church bells in the town of Dolores. He urged people to fight against the Spanish, who had ruled Mexico for 300 years. Mexico won its freedom on September 28, 1821, after the War of Independence. Today, people wave the Mexican flag and celebrate with huge parades, brilliant fireworks displays, and lively dancing. There are also rodeos, bullfights, and family fiestas with plenty of homemade food!

Fireworks are set off in front of the National Palace in Mexico City to celebrate Independence Day.

Day of the Dead

One of the most popular Mexican holidays is the Day of the Dead, or *Dia de los Muertos*. Part of a three-day festival from October 31 to November 2, the Day of the Dead honors people who have died and mixes Aztec and Catholic beliefs. Over these three days, it is believed that the souls of dead ancestors come back to visit and guide living relatives. People visit cemeteries and tend the graves of loved ones. They light candles and bring flowers and the dead person's favorite foods. Some people stay at the graveside all night. The skeleton symbol is everywhere, even in food! Candy skulls are popular, as is "bread of the dead," *pan de muerto*. In processions, people wear skeleton makeup and costumes.

DID YOU KNOW?

Partygoers from all over the world come to Mexico to celebrate the carnival in Mazatlán, on the west coast. It is the third largest carnival in the world, after those in New Orleans and Río de Janeiro.

Let's Cook!

Native Mexicans perform traditional dances at the annual Guelaguetza festival, in Oaxaca.

Local Fiestas

Mexicans love to celebrate! Local fiestas are held in every village, town, and city across the country. Some are in honor of a local saint, but some date back to before Christianity and celebrate the harvest or the coming of the rains. There are processions around the church, lively music, and fireworks. Native peoples do special dances in traditional costumes. Rodeos, bullfights, and carnival rides are also common. Delicious food is sold everywhere, and homemade food is cooked to share with family, friends, and neighbors.

DID YOU KNOW?

As part of the Holy Week celebrations, some people explode papier-mâché figures of Judas. This is because Judas betrayed Jesus, which led to his death.

Musicians play at the Holy Cross festival in Valle del Maiz, San Miguel de Allende, in central Mexico. It is held at the end of May each year.

 The Three Kings, or Wise Men, and baby Jesus dolls are on sale at a market for *Dia de Reyes* decorations.

Three Kings' Day

Although Christmas Day is celebrated in Mexico, it is on January 6—Three Kings' Day (*Dia de Reyes*)—that children receive gifts. The day honors the Three Wise Men who went to find Jesus after his birth. It is the wise men who hand out presents, not Santa Claus! A special cake called *rosca de reyes* is baked with a figurine of the baby Jesus inside. Whoever finds the figure must throw a party on February 2, Candlemas (*Día de la Candelaria*), another church holiday.

Holy Week Plays

In Mexico, each day of Holy Week (*Semana Santa*) leading up to Easter has a special celebration. It is popular for people to stage Passion Plays, where the last days of Jesus Christ are reenacted. There are processions on Good Friday, but Easter Day itself is celebrated quietly.

Actors reenact the life of Christ during a traditional Easter Passion Play procession in Tlalnepantla, in central Mexico.

Kings' Cake

Makes 1 cake

This fruitcake is baked to eat on *Dia de Reyes*, "Kings' Day," on January 6. It is a yeast cake that calls for candied fruit in Christmas colors.

YOU WILL NEED

- ✓ 4 cups all-purpose flour
- ✓ 1/3 of a 2-ounce cake of fresh yeast
- ✓ 3 tablespoons superfine sugar
- ✓ ½ cup warm milk
- ✓ ½ cup softened butter
- ✓ a pinch of salt
- ✓ grated zest of 1 organic orange
- ✓ grated zest of ½ organic lemon
- ✓ 4 ounces mixed candied fruit, plus more for decorating
- ✓ butter for greasing the cookie sheet
- ✓ 1 large egg

PLUS:
- ✓ a small baby doll or other small baby figure

1 Place a flour sifter over a large bowl. Add the flour, and sift it into the bowl. This will make the flour extra-fine. Make a hollow in the middle of the flour mound with a spoon.

2 Crumble the yeast into a small bowl or cup, and add 1 tablespoon sugar and all of the milk. Stir well, and pour the yeast mixture into the hollow in the flour. Sprinkle a little flour on top. Take a clean dishcloth and cover the bowl. Leave it to stand in a warm place for about 20 minutes.

3 Add the rest of the sugar, the softened butter, salt, and grated orange and lemon zest to the bowl. With clean hands, mix all the ingredients together. Knead the dough until it becomes smooth.

5 Preheat the oven to 350°F. Crack the egg, and separate the egg yolk from the white. Beat the yolk with a fork, and brush it over the cake. Press pieces of candied fruit into the dough for decoration. Bake the cake for 30 minutes, then remove it from the oven. Put it on a wire rack to cool.

DID YOU KNOW?

The baby figurine that is baked into the cake represents baby Jesus hiding from King Herod. Around the time Jesus was born, King Herod ordered that all male babies under the age of 2 should be killed.

4 Using a sharp knife, chop the candied fruit. Stir it into the dough. Push the baby Jesus figure into the dough. Shape the dough into a thick ring. Put a little butter on a piece of paper towel, and use it to grease a cookie sheet. Place the dough ring on the sheet, and cover it with a clean dishcloth. Leave it in a warm place for 30 minutes.

Tamales

Serves 4

This yummy dish is made with seasoned chicken and masa harina flour. It is wrapped in a corn husk and tied with string, then steamed!

YOU WILL NEED

- 4 cups masa harina flour
- 1 cup chicken stock
- salt, black pepper
- 3 ounces shortening
- 2–3 chiles
- 1 pound chicken breast, boned and skinned
- 1 onion
- 2 tablespoons oil
- 2 garlic cloves
- 1 small can tomatoes (14 ounces)
- ground cumin
- 1 handful fresh cilantro
- softened corn husks

1 Put the masa harina flour in a bowl, add the stock and salt, and stir together until it is a thick mixture. In a small skillet, melt the shortening and stir it into the mixture. When it has cooled down, knead the dough. Cover with a clean dishcloth, and set the dough aside.

2 Rinse, trim, and deseed the chiles (see page 13). Using a sharp knife, cut the chicken into very small cubes. Using a clean knife, peel and chop the onion (see page 13). Rinse the cilantro, shake it dry, and chop the leaves.

TOP TIP

Before you start cooking, put the corn husks into a bowl filled with warm water. Soak the husks for 1–2 hours to soften them. If you can't get any leaves, use aluminum foil instead, but don't soak it!

5 On a big plate, lay out the corn husks. Put 1½ tablespoons of corn dough on each leaf, and spread it using the back of a spoon. Place 1½ tablespoons of the chicken filling on top. Seal the dough over the chicken, then fold the husks over the dough—roll up one way, then turn up the sides, and tie with a piece of string.

6 Fill a large saucepan 2–3 inches deep with water, and bring to a boil. Line a steamer basket with more corn husks, and add the tamales. Put the basket in the saucepan, and cover. Simmer for 1 hour over low heat. The tamales are done when the husks come off easily.

3 Put the oil in a large saucepan, and gently heat. Add the chopped onion and fry for 5 minutes until it is golden, stirring constantly. Add the chicken and fry for 5 minutes, stirring, until the meat is brown all over.

SAFETY TIP

Always wash your hands with soap and warm water after handling raw chicken. Wash all cutting boards and utensils used to prepare raw chicken, too.

4 Peel the garlic. Push it through a garlic press over the saucepan. Stir in the chiles and tomatoes. Add the salt, cumin, and black pepper. Cook for a few minutes. Stir in the chopped cilantro.

Let's Cook!

Celebrating at Home

Mexicans celebrate religious feast days and family events with singing, dancing, and festive meals. Many people decorate their houses for special occasions.

Weddings

In Mexico, weddings are huge celebrations that include the couple's extended families, friends, and neighbors. The couple's "sponsors" help to plan and pay for the wedding, and promise to give advice on married life. Because almost 90 percent of Mexicans are Roman Catholic, the wedding usually takes place in a church to the sounds of a lively mariachi band. During the ceremony, the groom gives the bride 13 gold coins, symbolizing that he gives her his worldly goods and trusts her. A lasso of rosary beads is put around the couple's necks in a figure eight. This symbolizes that their lives are joined together. A big fiesta starts as soon as the church ceremony ends!

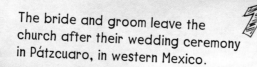

The bride and groom leave the church after their wedding ceremony in Pátzcuaro, in western Mexico.

28

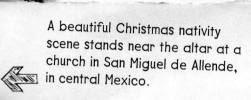
A beautiful Christmas nativity scene stands near the altar at a church in San Miguel de Allende, in central Mexico.

A traditional mariachi band performs on stage. Mariachi bands play the music at most weddings in Mexico.

Las Posadas

Christmastime brings many traditions in Mexico. Every night for nine nights before December 25, children take part in a candlelit procession called *Las Posadas*. They walk from door to door in the neighborhood or village, carrying a nativity crèche with figures of Joseph, Mary, and the baby Jesus. Knocking on each door, they sing songs until the family lets them in. This symbolizes the Holy Family being turned down at many inns until they finally reach the manger where Jesus is born. On Christmas Eve, fireworks are set off to announce Christ's birth. The *Las Posadas* tradition dates back to the 1500s and also has roots in an earlier Aztec winter solstice festival.

DID YOU KNOW?

Some brides wear a traditional Mexican wedding dress. Others wear a long white dress with a mantilla veil. Yellow, blue, and red ribbons are sewn into the bride's slip for good luck, so that there will always be food, money, and love!

Birthdays

In Mexico, family and friends gather for a huge birthday fiesta. No party would be complete without hitting the piñata, a papier-mâché animal with candy inside. People take turns hitting the brightly colored animal until it breaks apart and all the treats pour out. The birthday meal is prepared with foods such as tortillas with salsa, taquitos (rolled tacos), and burritos. Sweets include *arroz con leche* (Mexican rice pudding), caramel flan, and churros (a long doughnut). Traditionally, the birthday person's hands are tied behind his or her back as they take the first bite of the birthday cake—usually it gets squashed on their face!

A boy gets ready to hit an animal piñata at a birthday party. He is blindfolded to make it harder and more fun!

DID YOU KNOW?

Many Mexicans celebrate their name day as well as their birthday. A name day is the feast day of the saint a person is named after. So if your name is "Juan," you will celebrate St. John's day.

A Mexican girl gets ready to share her colorful Quinceañera birthday cake.

The Quinceañera

When a girl reaches the age of 15, she is considered to be a woman. The girl plans months ahead for the Fiesta Quinceañera ("party for 15 years"). She looks forward to the party with great excitement and chooses a beautiful dress and tiara. A mass is held in her honor at church, where she walks to the altar with her parents and a maid of honor. The girl offers flowers to the Virgin Mary, who represents womanhood in the church. Afterward, there is a huge party with lots of food, special gifts, and a special, lavishly decorated birthday cake!

Native Ceremonies

In Mexico, some Native peoples, such as the Maya and the Aztec, combine elements of their old religions with Catholicism. They perform ceremonies that start in church, with lit candles and pine needles strewn across the floor. Then they move outdoors to perform a ritual in the caves and mountains where their ancestors worshiped. Many Maya communities still have "day-keepers" who keep track of the ancient Maya calendar, which includes a schedule for special days.

A woman performs a traditional Maya ceremony. Many of the old rituals are still performed today.

piñata

Makes 1 Piñata

Birthdays in Mexico always mean hitting a piñata until it breaks and showers everybody with candy! This piñata takes a few days to make, so start early.

YOU WILL NEED

- 1 large, oval balloon
- two or three old newspapers
- white glue
- scissors or craft knife
- tape
- piñata patterns for the head and legs
- thin cardboard
- colored tissue paper

FOR THE FILLING:
- candies of your choice

1 Rip the newspapers into strips about 1 inch by 5 inches (2.5 cm x 12.5 cm). Pour the glue into an old bowl, and soak the paper strips in the glue. Blow up the balloon, and tie a knot at the end.

TOP TIP
Be sure to use wrapped candy to fill the piñata, so that it doesn't get stale or dusty before you play the game.

5 Fill the body of the piñata with candies through the hole left when you cut out the lid in Step 3. Afterward, carefully tape the lid in place.

6 To start the game, blindfold a player. Turn him or her around a few times and give them a stick. Point them in the right direction so they don't hit anyone! Each player may hit the piñata three times. When it breaks, share the goodies.

2 Place strips of gluey paper on the balloon, until the surface is covered. Leave to dry. Repeat this three more times, leaving each layer to dry.

3 With the help of an adult assistant, cut a lid in the side of the papier-mâché–covered balloon. Using the piñata pattern, draw around the outlines of the head and leg shapes onto thin cardboard, and cut out the shapes. Follow the instructions included with the piñata pattern to tape the head and legs to the balloon-shaped body.

4 Cut the colored tissue paper into strips about 1 inch by 2 inches (2.5 cm x 5 cm). Glue one end of each strip to the piñata, and let the other end hang loose. For the next row, overlap the strips like a row of roof tiles.

Piña Colada

Makes 4–6 cocktails

Many kinds of tropical fruit grow in Mexico, including the tangy pineapple used in this recipe. This is a nonalcoholic version of a famous cocktail.

YOU WILL NEED

- 1 small fresh pineapple
- 1 cup sweetened coconut cream
- 1 cup cold milk
- lots of crushed ice

DECORATIONS:
- pineapple slices
- long straws

1 Peel the green leaves off the pineapple. Chop off the top and bottom of the pineapple, so that it can stand upright by itself.

2 To cut off the thick skin, carefully slice down the sides of the pineapple. Slice the pineapple into quarters, from the top downward. Carefully cut out the hard center, and discard it. Cut the quartered pineapple into smaller pieces.

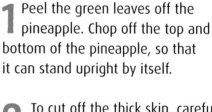

TOP TIP

Make crushed ice easily using an ice crusher. Just fill it with ice cubes, and turn the handle to crush the ice. If you don't have an ice crusher, put the ice cubes in a ziplock plastic bag, and place it on a hard surface. Pound the bag with a hammer or mallet.

5 Stir the pineapple puree into the coconut milk mix. Add crushed ice to some tall glasses, and pour the drink over the ice. Stick a pineapple chunk on each glass to decorate, and serve with a straw.

TOP TIP
You can buy fresh-sliced pineapple chunks from the store to save time preparing the pineapple.

3 Put a few pineapple chunks aside to use for the garnish. Put the other chunks into a blender, or blend them with a handheld blender, until they are smooth.

4 Put the coconut cream and the milk into a clean measuring cup. Using the handheld blender, mix them together until they foam a little.

Daily Life in Mexico

Life in Mexico's major cities revolves around industry and commerce. In the countryside, people farm the land using traditional methods. Wherever they live, **46 percent** of Mexicans live in poverty.

The Countryside

People live simply in the Mexican countryside. In small villages, many families work on nearby farms, and their children join in the work. In some Native American areas, houses are made of adobe—a kind of clay material hardened in the sun—with thatched roofs. Many Native peoples make and sell crafts that their families have made for centuries, such as reed figures, handwoven fabrics and clothes, and silver jewelry. Most villages have a church and a market that sells locally grown fruit and vegetables. People visit larger towns, which have more shops and national chain stores, if they want to buy other household goods.

A village market sells fresh produce from the surrounding farmland. People shop for fresh food in markets like this all across Mexico.

High-rise buildings spread out for miles across Mexico City. The city was built on the site of Tenochtitlán, the ancient Aztec capital that was destroyed by the Spanish in 1521.

City Life

Life in Mexico's urban areas is very busy. People in cities, such as Mexico City, Guadalajara, and Tijuana, work in industries including information technology, banking, textiles, shoes, medical equipment, and food processing. With over 20 million people, Greater Mexico City has a subway, buses, and trolley cars, but cars still cause massive air pollution. Wealthy neighborhoods sit alongside extremely poor areas, and thousands of homeless children roam the streets.

DID YOU KNOW?

Most Mexicans have ancestors who were a mix of Spanish and Native American. This is known as being of mestizo heritage. Native peoples today include the Náhuatl, Maya, Zapotec, Mixtec, and many others.

People sell goods at a busy street market on the Plaza de la Constitucion, in Mexico City.

Let's Cook!

Cowboys wave to cheering crowds at a rodeo show in Mexico. Rodeos came to the country from Spain in the 1500s.

Time Off

People are generally sociable in Mexico and like to spend time together. They often visit a local park, lake, or beach with friends and family, and take a picnic! They also visit museums and attend concerts or explore the ancient temples built by the Aztec and Maya. Soccer (*futbol*) is popular throughout Mexico. People play it in parks and in the streets, and enthusiastically follow the national team. Rodeos (*charradas*), where cowboys lasso and ride bulls, are another favorite pastime!

A family gathers for lunch, which is the biggest meal of the day. It is eaten mid-afternoon, followed by a siesta.

DID YOU KNOW?

Mexicans make a sauce called mole, which includes chiles, spices, tomatoes—and chocolate! It is often used in meat dishes.

School Days

Basic education in Mexico is free for all children. Between age three and five years, children may go to preschool. But starting at six years old, they must attend six years of primary school, followed by three years of junior high school. After that, children may stop attending school, but just over half go on to study three years of high school. The school day is split into two shifts—students attend either a morning or an afternoon shift. Because it is very hot in Mexico, a two-hour siesta, or rest break, is taken at 2:00 p.m.

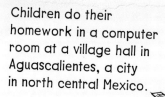
Children do their homework in a computer room at a village hall in Aguascalientes, a city in north central Mexico.

Mealtimes

Meals in Mexico are a chance to enjoy homemade food and share plenty of lively talk. Breakfast (*el desayuno*) is often just a sweet roll or fruit. Lunch (*la comida*) is the big meal of the day, eaten at around 2:00 p.m. It includes soup or salad, meat, seafood, or chicken and vegetables with rice or beans. A light supper (*la cena*), eaten at 8:00 p.m. or later, is usually just soup or tacos. Hot tortillas are eaten with almost every meal!

Eggs Rancheros

Serves 4

This egg and tortilla dish makes a wonderful, nutritious breakfast before school. It is quick and easy to make but best of all delicious!

YOU WILL NEED

FOR THE GARNISH:
- ✓ avocado and lime wedges
- ✓ crumbled feta
- ✓ fresh cilantro leaves

FOR THE TORTILLA DISH:
- ✓ 1 cup tomato salsa (from a jar)
- ✓ 4 wheat or corn tortillas
- ✓ 1 tablespoon butter or oil for frying
- ✓ 4 eggs
- ✓ 1/4 cup grated cheese (for example, cheddar)
- ✓ salt, pepper

1 Prepare the garnish first. Peel the avocado, scoop out the pit, and cut the flesh into wedges. Cut the lime into wedges, and squeeze one wedge over the avocado. Crumble the feta into a small bowl. Rinse and dry the cilantro leaves, and set aside.

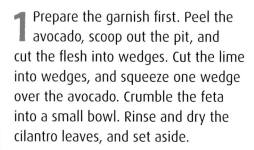

TOP TIP

To make your own salsa, heat 2 tablespoons oil in a skillet. Add 1 chopped onion and 1 crushed garlic clove. Fry for 5 minutes, stirring from time to time. Stir in 1 can (14 ounces) chopped tomatoes. Crumble five dried chiles, and add to mix with 1/2 teaspoon salt. Simmer for 10 minutes.

2 Add the salsa to a small saucepan, and simmer over low heat, stirring. Put each tortilla on an ovenproof plate, and heat in the microwave for 1 minute. Spread salsa over each hot tortilla.

4 Preheat the oven to 350°F. Sprinkle grated cheese on top of the tortillas. Season with a little salt and pepper.

5 Put the plates in the oven for 5 minutes, or until the cheese melts. Garnish with the avocado and lime wedges. Sprinkle with feta and cilantro.

3 Heat the butter or oil in a skillet over medium heat. Crack one egg into the pan, and fry it until it is set. Using a spatula, carefully lift out the egg, and place on top of the salsa.

DID YOU KNOW?

Eggs are a great source of high-quality protein. They also provide 18 vitamins and minerals. Use them in baking, cooking, or eat them on their own!

Black Bean Soup

Serves 4

Forget about canned soup—homemade bean soup is the best! This savory dish is a meal in itself, and it is surprisingly easy to make.

YOU WILL NEED

- 1½ cups canned black Mexican beans (or calypso beans or adzuki beans)
- 4 cups vegetable or chicken stock
- 2 green chiles
- 3 onions
- 2 garlic cloves
- 1 pound fresh tomatoes
- 4 tablespoons oil
- 1½ cups canned corn kernels
- a pinch of salt, black pepper
- 1 teaspoon ground cumin
- 2 tablespoons vinegar
- fresh cilantro leaves

1 Put the beans and the stock in a large saucepan, and simmer for around 10 minutes over low heat. Rinse, trim, and deseed the chiles (see page 13). Peel and chop the onions (see page 13) and the garlic.

2 Put the tomatoes in a bowl. Cover with boiling water. Leave them for 1 minute. Drain and cover them with cold water. When cooled, drain and remove the skins. Cut out the stems and discard, and chop the flesh.

4 Let the beans cool a little, and ladle half the beans and their liquid into a blender, and blend them. Return the blended beans to the other beans. Stir in the onions and garlic.

5 Add a few tablespoons of cold water if the soup is too thick, and stir well. Taste to check the seasoning, then simmer the soup over low heat. Ladle into bowls, sprinkle with the cilantro leaves, and serve.

3 Heat the oil in a large saucepan, and add the chopped onion and garlic. Fry for 5 minutes, or until transparent (see-through). Add the chiles, the chopped tomatoes, and the corn. Sprinkle in the salt, pepper, cumin, and vinegar. Stir to combine all the ingredients.

TOP TIP

You can use dried beans for an even better flavor. Soak ½ cup dried beans in 1½ cups water for six hours. Cook the beans in a heavy metal saucepan for 1½ hours, and use in the recipe.

RECIPE: Let's Cook!

Mexican Rice

Serves 4

This yummy rice dish makes a quick, tasty meal. You can add pretty much any chopped vegetable, such as peas, corn, zucchini, or cooked eggplant.

YOU WILL NEED

- 4 pounds beefsteak tomatoes
- 3 onions
- 5 garlic cloves
- 3 cups vegetable stock
- 1 tablespoon tomato paste
- 2 cups long-grain rice
- 2 carrots
- 1 green bell pepper
- salt, pepper
- fresh cilantro leaves

1 Make a slash in the top of each tomato, and plunge them into a bowl of boiling water for 1 minute. Lift them out with a slotted spoon and cool in cold water. Remove the skins, and roughly chop the flesh.

2 Peel and roughly chop the onions and garlic cloves (see page 13). Put the onion, garlic, and tomatoes in a blender, and blend together until smooth.

3 Put the stock in a large saucepan, and stir in the tomato paste. Add the tomato, onion, and garlic mixture. Simmer until the mixture boils. Add the rice and stir well, bringing the pan to a boil again. Cover the saucepan, and simmer for 10 minutes.

4 Rinse the carrots, and scrape them clean. Rinse the bell pepper, cut it in half, and scrape out the seeds. Slice the carrots and the pepper into long strips, then slice them into small cubes.

5 Add the carrot and pepper cubes to the rice in the saucepan. Stir everything to combine. Cover with the lid, and cook for another 10 minutes.

6 Check to see if all the ingredients are done. The vegetables should be a little crunchy. Taste and adjust the seasoning. Put the rice in a bowl, sprinkle with cilantro leaves, and serve.

DID YOU KNOW?

Rice was brought to Mexico by the Spanish in the 1500s. It has become a staple in the Mexican diet and is used in soups, main dishes, and sweet desserts.

Glossary

avocado The fruit of a tree native to Mexico, with creamy, green flesh.

cacao The beanlike seed from which cocoa and chocolate are made. Its origins are in Mexico. It was introduced to the rest of world by the Spanish.

carnival Festivities held before Lent, usually in late February or early March.

fiesta In Spanish-speaking countries, a religious festival or an event with celebrations and festivities, such as dancing and parades.

guacamole A dip made with mashed avocados, chiles, lemon or lime juice, onions, tomatoes, and spices.

mariachi A traditional musical band that plays at weddings and festivals.

masa harina A flour made from corn, or maize, used to make tortillas.

piñata A large, hollow papier-mâché object containing candies and gifts.

posadas A traditional carol-singing walk made each night for nine days leading up to Christmas.

quinceañera A girl's fifteenth birthday, when she is said to become a woman. She and her family attend mass, and a huge party is thrown in her honor.

rosca de reyes Kings' Cake, made for Three Kings' Day, or the Epiphany. The cake has a figurine of the baby Jesus baked into it.

salsa Any kind of sauce, but often a spicy dip made with tomatoes, chile, onions, and cilantro.

Semana Santa Holy Week, the week before Easter, celebrated in Mexico with processions and Passion Plays that reenact Christ's last days on Earth.

siesta A rest or nap taken in the afternoon during the hottest hours of the day in places with a hot climate.

tamales A dish made with meat and vegetables wrapped in cornmeal, then wrapped in corn husks and steamed.

tortilla A thin, round flatbread made from masa harina flour. Hot tortillas are eaten with almost every Mexican meal.

Further Resources

Books

DK Publishing.
Aztec, Inca & Maya (DK Eyewitness Books).
DK Publishing, New York: 2011.

Kramme, Michael.
Mayan, Incan, and Aztec Civilizations.
Mark Twain Media, Greensboro, NC: 2012.

Petrillo, Valerie.
A Kid's Guide to Latino History: More than 50 Activities.
Chicago Review Press, Chicago: 2009.

Roman, Carole P.
If you were me and lived in ... Mexico: A Child's Introduction to Cultures Around the World.
CreateSpace Independent Publishing, Charleston, NC: 2013.

Websites

Due to the changing nature of Internet links, PowerKids Press has developed an online list of websites related to the subject of this book. This site is updated regularly. Please use this link to access the list:

www.powerkidslinks.com/lc/mexico

Index